The All-Star Administrative Professional

Dr. Susan Harrison

While every precaution has been taken in the preparation of this book, the publisher assumes no responsibility for errors or omissions, or for damages resulting from the use of the information contained herein.

THE ALL-STAR ADMINISTRATIVE PROFESSIONAL

First edition. October 19, 2020.

Copyright © 2020 Dr. Susan Harrison.

Written by Dr. Susan Harrison.

Introduction

Let's get right to the point: You know where the bodies are buried. You know all the secrets—where the files and supplies are stored, and even the super-secret method of changing the toner. You know how to talk to all kinds of vendors, and which are worth remembering (and you do remember them). You are the gatekeeper and don't allow anyone to speak to or meet your boss without your approval. You know which employees to ask for things three months in advance due to their procrastination habit, and who to ask for things only two weeks early because they love the thrill of having little time. You know who not to approach before she has had her coffee. Yes, my friend, you know it all. When you are out sick, you get 100 calls a day asking where things are and when things are supposed to happen.

You are an administrative professional.

According to the U.S. Department of Labor, there are nearly four million administrative assistants at work today in the United States. Four million! The list of industries you populate is as long as your arm—from healthcare and education, to finance and non-profits, and everything in between. Anyone who doesn't have an assistant wishes she did. Some admins are just meh, and some, my friends, are all-stars.

So what makes an all-star? They are professionals at conversation, writing, conflict resolution, delegating, system optimization, meeting deadlines, public relations, prioritization, continuing education, healthy relationships, and much more. They are confident, resilient, hard workers with great attitudes. Does that describe you?

All-star admins know they are professionals and act accordingly. They know their job matters. They know they matter. I have met many admins in my workshops around the country who say things like, "I'm just an admin," as if this isn't a real job or as important or needed as other jobs. You are not a JUST! You are as important as any other cog in the wheel of your workplace. And once you recognize that fact and begin to act as the valuable asset you are, success and satisfaction will naturally increase, not only for yourself, but also for those around you.

I know some of you don't believe that yet. You still think you are a *just*. You look around your office and think you don't have a real job, one that is important or as needed as other professions. Okay, you aren't as needed as firefighters, police officers, or heart surgeons, but neither are most of us. Come to think of it, even the medical field has its hierarchy. You can bet the general surgeon who just saved the life of a kid with a burst appendix doesn't go home at night thinking, "I sure wish someday I could be a brain surgeon. They are the real difference-makers in the world."

You matter as much as anyone in your company. Take away all of the admins and let's see if anyone can find the extra paper for the copier. Of course that is a joke and not a joke. In my conversations, I've learned that many people in an office do not know basic things like where the paper is stored, or, heaven forbid, how to tweak the copy machine. You not only know how to fix it most of the time, but who to call when you can't. You know how to get what you want and can run circles around anyone when it comes to organizing schedules. You keep your boss most productive by understanding her needs and knowing who will just be wasting her time. And when your boss is having a bad day, you know to steer clear! You know how to organize a meeting with the best of them. You can handle the RSVPs, location, catering, speaker, and every detail down to the color of the tablecloths—and come in under budget.

Are you thinking, *Well, anyone can do those things.* You are absolutely wrong. Let me tell you about my friend Stacy. She has a college degree, is creative, and wonderful at her job but has never been able to handle numbers or keep things organized. The first time she was tasked to balance the books at her office, she asked her supervisor how close it had to be, as in, can she be a dollar off, or a nickel? Her boss could not believe she even asked the question! No! You have to be exact! These are numbers! Another time at a trade show, she oversold a tour bus and left her boss apologizing and refunding money on the spot. I would not want her to be in charge of any office budget, or handling money anywhere! Not everyone can be an admin, and certainly not everyone can be an all-star admin.

So are you ready to shoot for the stars? Are you feeling a little puny and needing encouragement or wisdom? You have picked up the right book! After speaking for years in front of administrative professionals' groups all around the country, working one-on-one with them, and being one myself, I have learned all about the ins and outs of office support. With lots of time logged speaking with admins, their bosses, and coworkers about the good and bad of office life, I am fully prepared to coach you into the Administrative Assistant Hall of Fame. Let's get started!

All-Star Attitude

Now that you understand your worth, let's talk about the all-star attitude. If we were face-to-face in a workshop, I would ask you why attitude matters. Stop for a moment and consider the question. Does attitude matter? Why yes, more or less.

Here's the more:

· A good attitude will get you more cooperation from coworkers, supervisors, and clients.

· A good attitude will help you gain respect and give you a larger voice when you have something to say.

· A good attitude will increase your confidence.

· A good attitude will give you more energy. (That is a scientific fact. Look it up.)

· A good attitude will give you credibility when a conflict arises.

· A good attitude will open doors and draw even more positivity into your life.

Optimism will also foster more success for you, and I am living proof of that. Many years ago, I was promoted within a month of starting a new job. The people who had been hoping for that promotion, those who had been there a long time and were still telling me where things were, hated me after that. They knew more than me and they knew they knew more than me. The promotion came because of my attitude. I was positive, smiled, and enjoyed learning and helping. The clients enjoyed me because I made them feel special and liked. The employees who didn't get promoted didn't do anything beyond their job description, didn't act like they enjoyed the job, and were a bit intimidating to deal with.

This is not an isolated incident. Over and over I have been promoted quickly because of my attitude. I'm not really anything special (although my mom would disagree), I just choose positivity. And it's not just me! My friend Jim always has a smile on his face. He recently took on a new job after being recruited by a friend at the company, and within the first month that friend was answering to him! Over and over you will see positive people being promoted quickly.

So what's the *less* when it comes to a positive attitude? Less stress! Physically, emotionally, mentally, and spiritually, you will be less drained at the end of a day full of upbeat thoughts and words.

Let's be real. We all know that one person who has a bad attitude and it brings us down. We are intimidated to go up and ask for something because we are fearful that we will get our heads bitten off, or at the very least be spoken to rudely, as if we don't matter. We avoid that person when at all possible.

How do you know if you have a good or bad attitude? I can guarantee the person who comes to your mind when I say Negative Nellie has no idea she is a drain on the world's joy. You would think we each have a good handle on our own thought patterns, but in reality most of us do not. Although I have always been complimented for being positive, several years ago my thought patterns began to devolve and I did not even realize it. Fortunately, during that time an old friend called me and almost immediately said, "You've changed. You sound negative." Right away I became defensive and said, "No, I'm not." (Haven't I always been defined by my positivity?) We continued the conversation but I could not stop thinking about what he said. It really bothered me, which is when I knew some truth might be there, so I began examining my thoughts. It wasn't long before I realized he was right! What?! I had always been the most positive person I know! What happened? Well, I spent a lot of time with a negative person and thought my positivity would rub off, but instead the negativity rubbed off on me and I wasn't even aware. Complaining, gossiping, nit picking, arguing, and overall negativity had become my new normal.

But it wasn't too late. I spent time noticing my thoughts and began questioning them. I started thinking before I spoke and didn't say things that could possibly be seen as negative. For example, when I walked into a cold room, I didn't say, "I'm cold," but instead put on a sweater or asked to get the temperature changed. I did not complain. It really isn't bad to say when a room is cold but I needed to reprogram my brain. The best way to do that was to not say anything remotely negative. This made me hyper aware. After about a week, the negative thoughts started going away. It took some concentration at first, but before long I was back to my old self. I still must be vigilant about my thoughts, but positivity is once again my normal mode of operation.

If you have the courage to ask a good friend about your attitude you will probably get an honest answer. If you don't have any friends like that, do a self-evaluation. If you suspect you are an Eeyore, you probably are. Monitor your thoughts. This is more than making a hashmark every time something pessimistic comes to mind. Even if you aren't actively grousing, are you actively being thankful? Take the simple example of room temperature. Do you notice it only when it's uncomfortable? How about being thankful when it's nice, thankful that you have a sweater when it's cold, and thankful for ice cream when it's hot (being thankful for ice cream is always a good idea). Practice gratefulness like you practice any sport or musical instrument.

Pop culture is brimming with messages of self-acceptance, and rightfully so. But that message is not, "I don't care if anyone likes me." If you are saying that yourself, you are not happy and those around you are not happy. It will likely not improve (or even maintain) your career, health, or love life. That kind of "I don't care" comment is over the top. You should care if someone likes you, but if no one seems to, it's not too late to make changes. I'll tell it to you straight: If no one likes you, you are the problem.

One idea to help improve the situation is to review your online habits. Studies have shown that social media, the twenty-four-hour news cycle, and plain old too much screen time has a horrible effect on our outlook and even our health. These negative outcomes are due to many factors, including discontent (Who hasn't had beach photo envy?), lost productivity, fear mongering, and the physiological aspect of screens, blue light, and the way this is reprogramming our brains and our society. I recently heard about a posh New York restaurant that brings a box to the table and asks all guests to leave their phones in the box for the duration of their meal. Another idea I heard was to pile phones in the middle of the table and the first person to touch theirs has to pick up the check. (That sounds a little unsanitary, but you can work something out.) I think the best idea is to put your phones away when at the dinner table or a gathering of friends or family. Just seeing it can spark a psychological reaction of wondering if you are missing out on something. FOMO anyone?

Hot Tip: If you have never reviewed your online presence, do it today. You may be amazed at what comes up when you type your name in an online search. Adjust social media privacy settings as high as you can and delete anything that could possibly reflect on you negatively in your personal or professional circles.

All-Star Appearance

Ready for more truth about what might need to change for you to become an all-star? Let's dive right into the most personal subjects first!

How you dress is a reflection of the kind of work others think you can do. This is one area where it does matter what people think of you. If you appear sloppy, then you may be less trusted with important clients or projects. I know a woman who does not care in the least what she looks like and it shows. She has had a very hard time through the years getting jobs and she doesn't understand why. Her background and knowledge are impressive, however, her appearance is not. She is over middle age, not in great shape, and wears belly shirts, tight pants, and does not seem to comb her hair. It is doubtful that comes even close to describing you, but I am asking you to take a hard look at your appearance because it could be holding you back. You do not have to be thin to look presentable, but you need to dress for your size. And belly shirts are never a good idea for an office. Neither are ill-fitting clothes or plunging necklines.

One day I had an appointment at a local coffee shop with a woman who owned her own business. She was dressed in clothes that did not fit and were covered with lint. Her hair was not washed and had a big tuft of it wadded up in the back as if it had never been combed. She also did not smell good, which we will address here in a bit. This woman was asking for my business and came to this meeting as I described. Needless to say, I was surprised. She turned out to be very nice and knowledgeable, although I admit when I saw her my first thought was I had no desire to work with her. But after getting to know her more, we did work together and she did a great job. However we cannot count on others giving us the benefit of the doubt.

Although I have not seen it myself, I have heard many stories about admins wearing fishnet stockings, short skirts, and/or much-too-revealing blouses. When I first began hearing these stories, I almost didn't believe them, but after hearing them for so long I know dressing like this is a real thing and a real problem. But what can it hurt? Aren't you just expressing yourself? It can hurt your credibility, reputation, pay, promotions, and relationships. Those things are too serious to not consider how your dress affects them.

Appearance doesn't stop at monitoring your standard of dress. If your spouse regularly picks pet hair or lint off your shirt or tucks in errant tags, take five extra seconds in front of the mirror each morning. Five seconds! Like it or not, your boss is less likely to hand over a detail-oriented project to someone whose got lipstick on her teeth or is sporting what I lovingly call "nap head" (although I do love my naps).

Your facial expressions are a big part of your appearance. There have been numerous admins I've met who have what is called Resting B*tch Face (RBF). It is the expression on your face when you are just sitting there or concentrating, and you look like you are upset. If you don't have it, chances are good you just thought of someone who does and intimidates coworkers. Here's one way to know. Do people ask you if you are okay? Do you get asked to smile? If so, you might have it. It can be a blessing! If you are working really hard on a project and don't want to be bothered, people will steer clear. Mostly though, it can hurt relationships so it's good to be aware of it. All it takes is to make a habit of having a little smile on your face while working so you look approachable.

One critical area of appearance is odor. Is there someone at your office you can still smell after you have been home for hours—either their cologne or their body odor? If you spray more than a few spritzes in the morning you are probably offending someone during the day. You may even be causing allergies to worsen for workmates. Some workplaces, like medical offices, go as far as to ban scents. Hopefully if you are an over-sprayer someone will be honest with you, but that doesn't usually happen. Ask a trusted friend, and change your behavior if they tell you that you stink. At more than one workshop I have heard stories about coworkers who would get up from their work area and no one would go near it due to the lingering smell. I'll never forget the story of a young man who smelled so bad but no one wanted to say anything to him. Finally, when someone asked him about it they found out he was homeless. People pulled together and helped him, and his life changed forever.

And if you go the gym in the morning, make sure you bring deodorant, and leave enough time to cool down so your blouse doesn't stick to your back all through the first meeting of the day. If you don't wear deodorant and think that's okay, think again. If you have gone through puberty, you need deodorant.

If you wear glasses, here's a free tip: Make sure to clean them every day. Just do it. How many of you know that person whose glasses are so gross you can't understand how they can see anything? Also, men, trim those nose and ear hairs. I know, extra hairs don't seem to be in most books about administrative assistants, but this is not most books. It's all about the details, people! If you demonstrate care in getting yourself ready for the day, you not only feel better, but others will be more comfortable around you.

Above all, be happy with yourself. Change the things you can and want to, and let go of the rest. We all want to lose (or gain) ten pounds, right? Work on it or let it go! Either way, stop talking about it. Believe me, your friends and family are tired of hearing about it! I went through a long period where I wouldn't wear short sleeves because I hated my arms. When my grown niece suggested a particular shirt while we were shopping, I told her about my aversion. She then changed my thinking by telling me that these were in fact my arms, so I should embrace them. It's really okay if no one likes them, and if they make me that unhappy I can change them!

Hot Tip: Use the brightest lighting possible in your dressing area. If you are overdoing the blush or your lace panties are showing through those new sheer white slacks, you want to spot it at home and not in the mirror at work.

All-Star Branding

Businessdictionary.com defines branding as "the process involved in creating a unique name and image for a product in the consumers' mind…" For our purposes here, you are the product and your boss, workmates, and clients are the consumers. From the first meeting, you began a process of creating a unique name and place for yourself at your office. This began with your appearance (hope those nose hairs were trimmed!), but it goes far beyond that. Let me give you an example.

Are you the office mom? The office mom is the woman (yes, I say woman because I haven't found a man who does it) who tends to everyone's needs; she makes us feel warm and good and even brings us home baked treats. She tells us everything will be okay, keeps the break room microwave clean, the copy paper filled and keeps candy on hand. We know we can leave our coffee cups in the sink because she will take care of them. I love having an office mom, I just don't want to be one. Maybe you are one and you love it. It makes you feel good and you like knowing you are helping to make our lives easier. That's wonderful. However, at least think about any possible effects. If you are consistently being passed over for promotions and the projects you want, it may be because you are considered a pushover, which may be due to being the office mom. Don't change if you don't want to—this book is not your boss, but now you know the risks.

One thing you don't want to do is brand yourself as the "ice woman." We all need to do things beyond our job description, but one woman in my workshop described herself as this way. Thinking that meant she was viewed as not a nice person, I was surprised she shared her brand. Then she went on to explain she was responsible for getting the ice. They had a fountain drink machine (which as a side note is pretty cool), and it needed the ice filled during the day. Instead of each person just getting ice when needed, they would stop by her desk and ask her to refill it. That was her brand. That was how people saw her, mainly because she stopped what she was doing each time and refilled it. Ice wasn't the only thing—she was also paper filler, coffee filler, toner changer, and more. It is surprising she got her regular work done. She admitted that was often a problem.

What was my advice? First, check with your boss to see if this is what she wants you to do. If she does, you can discuss it. If she doesn't, then the "ice woman" can stop doing the extra things. Next, how do you change? If it is something everyone can do like the ice and coffee, then you tell them you aren't going to be able to do that and ask them to do it. This will need to be repeated. You can even say, "Sarah (the boss) would like me to have other people fill the ice now." There is no need to be rude, just factual.

If it is something the person doesn't know how to do, then train her. Go with her to the copy machine and have her change the toner while talking her through it. Ask her to take notes. "I'll go with you and show you how." Or if you get resistance like this, "I don't have time, can you just do it for me?" "No, I can't but it won't take long."

What if it is someone with higher authority regularly demanding you perform tasks not in your job description? This may be the most important time to practice branding yourself as a professional, but use your discretion. Always defer to your boss.

Are you reading this and thinking, *this would never be me*? She is not you, but be mindful because it can be easy to start doing things at home and work and suddenly realize there is no reason you are the only one doing them. Or she may not be as assertive as you. And if this is you, don't feel silly for doing these things because it's not too late to stop.

You are responsible for how others in the office see you, what your brand looks like to them. Take a good hard look at your time spent each day and make sure you are presenting yourself to consumers (bosses, coworkers, clients) in the most positive light possible.

Hot Tip: Ask one or two of your close work friends to describe your office persona in a few words. Then ask your family to do the same. If you find a consistent negative connotation or even a non-productive trademark, make an effort to change your brand. If you have no idea how to accomplish that, hire a personal coach or even a therapist.

Bonus Hot Tip: If your time disappears and you don't know where it went, keep a daily log. You'll only need to do it a few days but it will help you see where your time is going.

All-Star Relationships

One complaint that all millionaires have is they never know who their true friends are. (Hard to feel too sorry for them, isn't it?) When the professional football players sign those multi-million-dollar contracts, old friends and cousins come out of the woodwork needing favors. When Instagram influencers hone their brand to the point they are making big bucks, the scammers love to take shots at them.

My point here is that once you realize you are an office treasure, have your brand recognized as highly valuable, and begin to act accordingly, there will be those who want to use you for their own personal advancement. We will call them the flatterers. They will tell you your idea to advance the schedule on the current project is wonderful, and then go to your boss and tear it apart. They will fill out the dreaded "anonymous" suggestion card and complain about how rough the toilet paper is when everyone knows you choose the TP vendor. Some want to get ahead at your expense. Some are just mean.

On the other end of that spectrum is Mindy. Everyone needs a Mindy. Mindy is an all-star admin when it comes to relationships (and well, everything). Let me explain. When I was pursuing my doctoral studies there was a wonderful admin in my department named Rhonda. Just kidding, her name was Mindy. She and I loved each other, as in hugs and long conversations about what was going on in our lives, loads of laughter, texts, checking up on each other, just BFF things. She made me feel special and important. Then one day I noticed she had a similar one-of-a-kind relationship with, well, *everyone*. Others shared similar stories about Mindy. She made them feel special, had private jokes, shared with them her Mtn. Dew obsession, gave special tips and stories for doctoral survival and treated them as very close friends, which they were. She was always sincere, without any agenda, and just loved people. Sure, I'm a bit jealous but mostly happy that others got to experience the Mindy love. If your job description requires you to work in an office with people, be a Mindy and everyone will love you too.

And don't forget relationships with those outside your office. Even if you love your job and can't imagine ever leaving, you need to make connections with others both in person and through online sources. Join a professional association or two and take a lunch hour or evening once in a while to connect with others in your city who walk in your shoes. Join Toastmasters and conquer your fear of public speaking. Join a book club. Get involved in Meetup.com. Get active in a church or your neighborhood association. Knowing more people will make your job easier and we all need connections!

Are you tired of hearing the phrase, "At the end of the day"? I know I am. But just this once, it really applies. At the end of the day, you go home, wherever that is, to whomever you go home to (including fur babies). It may be your burgeoning young family, your empty nest, your bachelor pad, or your mom's basement (no judgment here). If that environment is steeped in stress, fear, anger, financial worry, or any other negativity, it will affect your job performance.

The first step is to stop talking about it. Your coworkers are tired of hearing about it but really, the biggest reason to stop is that talking about it makes it more real. Let's say you have a fight with your husband before leaving for work. When you arrive, all you do is talk about how Charlie was on your last nerve. Instead of letting it go, you focus on it more and the more you focus on it, the more upset you are and the less you can fully concentrate on work. And then when you get home—poor Charlie!

The second step is to deal with anything that continually keeps coming up. Did you know that things don't tend to get resolved by ignoring them? At least that used to be the way I handled my issues. But how about instead you work on making them better. Depending on the situation, there are things you can do. A lot of issues can get better if we look at them more positively and become aware of our own part in making them into problems.

If what you are going through is serious such as a family illness, most bosses will give a little grace, but you still want to handle it professionally as much as possible. Talk to your boss privately about your situation and ask for help with extra time off, more work hours, or perhaps a flexible schedule. And speaking of your boss, don't miss the special section at the end of the book focusing on this complex relationship.

Hot Tip: Relationship maintenance can be overwhelming for a professional woman! If a lack of energy to touch base with friends and family is creating stress in your life, make a contact schedule. Create a list of your valuable relationships and write down on your calendar to call your mom or to meet your best friend for dessert on a regular basis. If it's not on your calendar for the day, you can let that guilt go!

All-Star Conversation

Do you know anyone who speaks in circles? Or are you someone who turns every conversation into a novella, talking in great detail around the point, and taking forever to get to the point? Let me give you an example:

"You know how I like to get things done around here? Well, Tammy works at her own pace and I understand that and how she needs to work. She is pretty busy with her three kids and her husband who works long hours. But I don't meet my deadlines. Tammy needs to get me her reports by Thursday, but I know she's busy with a full life and all, it's just that I need to get the reports because I have to not only check them but I also have to send them out to multiple people, you know, because you are one of them. So, I am not sure what to do about getting these reports so I can get my work done."

Are you tired after reading that? I'm tired after writing it, but I hear people talking like that all the time. What's the issue? Perhaps nothing, depending on the audience. If you are talking to your friend with time to kill and she loves your stories, then it's fine. If it's a coworker or boss who is busy and wants you to get to the point, it isn't.

If you are the circle talker, become more self-aware. (In fact, the topic of self-awareness is something you'll read about often in this book.) How do you know if you are draining energy and productive time from others? Ask yourself these questions:

· Do you always feel like people are cutting you off during conversation?

· Do people fail to maintain eye contact with you, either multi-tasking or doing something as rude as looking at their phone while you are talking? (And yes, unless your child is in surgery it is rude to look at your phone—or smartwatch—while having a conversation. It can wait two minutes, for Pete's sake.)

• When you tell someone you need five minutes of their time, is it always at least twice that before the conversation is over?

If you answered yes to any of these then you are probably a circle talker. Next time just state what you want and then explain it if necessary. You may even need to write down or at least rehearse exactly what you are going to say. If you are asked to elaborate, monitor yourself and watch the other person's body language and eye contact. Pay attention and then each time get better about getting to the point.

If you work with a circle talker, it's all about boundaries. When Kari needs to talk, tell her you have five minutes. At the five-minute mark, it may seem rude, but interrupt her and say with a smile something like, "Kari, I have to cut you off because I really only had five minutes. I have to finish this project I'm working on now. Maybe we can talk again later." You may even want to hold out your hand with all fingers up giving her a visual cue that the five minutes have passed. Don't make it an obnoxious high five, just a low-key reminder. With someone like this, repetition is the key. She has to know you mean it when you say five minutes. When you can, give this lengthy talker a bit more time and then she will be more likely to understand when you say five minutes, you mean it.

A few years back I had a small workshop with only five people. There was a participant who told a story about her boss, Andrew. She had trouble getting him to take a meeting with her but finally got one. A few minutes into the conversation, her boss pulled out his phone while she was talking and began texting. She couldn't believe how rude he was, and we were pretty much in shock as we listened. She continued her story and said then a man walked in and asked, "Andrew, do you have a few minutes to chat?" Andrew, her boss, looked at her and then said to the man, "sure" and left. He actually walked out of the meeting. After she finished, we expressed our dismay at how he behaved. Days later I gave it more thought and remembered that she was a circle talker. I'm not excusing the rude behavior of the boss, but I do understand why he did not want to listen. He should have been more assertive, however if she was more self-aware, this may have gone differently.

Another time I met with a woman at a local restaurant about her possibly doing some marketing for me. Let me make this clear: She wanted my business. She then spent time talking about herself including all of her history and illnesses in great detail. I don't mind hearing about people and their lives but she didn't ask me one question about me or what I like or what I needed. It took only about five minutes for me to understand that I couldn't get a word in so I just sat there and smiled and nodded occasionally. After an hour (yes, an hour!) of being polite, I reached my end so I went to the bathroom and washed my hands, just to get away. When I returned I didn't even sit but told her I needed to go. I left nicely but I didn't want to hear anything else. People are typically not aware how they come across in conversation, so if you are, you are way ahead of the crowd! And if you are not, you can make changes now. Ask yourself if everyone you talk to walks away knowing many, many things about your health, family life, and latest conflict with a friend. If you even hesitate there, ask yourself what you learned about the last person you spoke with. If the answer is nothing, you may be an over-sharer like the woman mentioned above. That needs to stop.

While we are on the subject of self-awareness in conversation, know any close talkers? Close talkers are not self-aware of space. If you back up from a close talker, he often moves even nearer and you begin a little dance. If it makes you uncomfortable there is no harm in pointing it out—he probably doesn't even realize he's doing it. Honest feedback is a special gift if you give it with kindness.

Let me change this up a bit. If you are trying to build rapport with someone who is a close talker, stay still. This will help the other person feel comfortable and more relaxed with you. This will stretch your conversation skills and keep your mind from wandering. It might even build a relationship.

Pay attention. Do people back away from you when you are having a one-on-one conversation? This may be because you're a close talker, or it may simply be your breath. If someone backs up from you, the first question to ask yourself is, "Do I need a mint?" I've offered so many mints to people who desperately needed one but didn't take it, until I finally learned to be specific. "Would you like a mint?" "No, thank you." "Take the mint," I say with a little head nod and sly smile. Unless you already have one in your mouth, TAKE THE MINT. If you had Italian last night or coffee this morning, you have bad breath. Guaranteed.

For the all-star admin, this is about communication and building rapport, not only with your boss and coworkers, but with vendors and clients as well. Did you know building rapport is not about you? It's about the other person! We tend to communicate with others the way we want them to speak to us. Let me illustrate. I once had a double date with another couple and all was going great for a while. They were nice and we were having pleasant conversation. Then the husband started talking about the company they wanted us to get involved in. To be fair, I knew this would be part of the evening but when I asked some questions, the husband became aggressive with his tone of voice and body language. He did not like me questioning the company he loved. When his body language finally became obnoxious (pointing and towering over me), I lit on fire. I leaned in and gave severe eye contact and backed him off me by saying things like, "Don't point your finger in my face" or something like that. I never yelled, but raised my voice to an uncomfortable level. I made my date uncomfortable and pretty much made it impossible for the four of us to get together again.

Fast-forward about six months and we were enjoying time with another couple. You guessed it, this husband also began pressuring us to get involved in the same company. He began by telling me he knew all about my last conversation with the other man. He got a little aggressive with his body language, warning me not to judge this opportunity. This time I decided to stay cool, understanding that this man was passionate but not finger pointing aggressive and that I wanted this to end better. I kept the eye contact consistent and even leaned in a bit. My mouth stayed pretty much shut and I just listened. It took about fifteen minutes, but I remained patient and refused to get overly excited. My blood pressure did not go up and I felt much more comfortable with how that evening ended.

What was the difference? I took control of the only thing I can control—myself. I decided that rather than to deal with someone as they were dealing with me, I would do the opposite. Does the Golden Rule ring a bell with anyone here? If we treat others as we wish to be treated, we may still have negative interactions, but we will avoid lots of regrets.

And let's face it, there will always be those with a communication style you just can't embrace.

The challenge is to figure out how others like to be communicated with, not just how you like to communicate. If you are loud and someone else is quiet, try and tone it down so she will be more receptive. Or if you like to get right down to business in the beginning of the day but someone else wants to chat for a few minutes about her weekend, go ahead and chat.

What about that all-important conversation—how do you successfully ask for a raise? In today's workplace many, many conversations that would have transpired face-to-face even a couple years ago are done by written messaging. Asking for a raise via email is a recipe for disaster!

This all-important negotiation should be handled in real time, with voices and, if possible, faces.

It's important to make an appointment with your boss for this conversation. If you are his admin, you probably handle the calendar, so this is an easy step. Just stick your name in a 15-minute slot. No need to list the "why" unless he asks. This conversation is all about timing. Consider your boss's temperament and what else is going on that day. Pick a slot where he will, for example, still be feeling good after meeting with an important client. Or after his morning coffee. Don't schedule yourself right after he is disciplining someone or when he's busy trying to catch up after a vacation.

I can't state this clearly enough—come prepared. Spend some time collecting data to prove why you are worth more than your current salary. Add up all the money you have saved the company with your savvy purchasing changes, note that you have not missed one deadline or come in late once. Remind him of the extra mile you went all those times you stayed late to work on key projects. Make this very specifically about you and resist the urge to let him know you know Tom makes a dollar an hour more than you.

Ask for a realistic (with a little stretch), firm number. Then wait. Use the salesman's simple tip that the first person to speak in a negotiation loses. It might go something like this (after you list your reasons for being so awesome): "So Mike, with those things in mind I would like to see my hourly rate raised to $20." Quiet. Wait for it. Wait for it. Don't even inhale! Let Mike be the next to speak and your chances of banking more cash goes way up.

Hot Tip: Today's workplace requires an ever increasing number of video and audio recordings of conversations, meetings, and presentations. How do you sound? Make a recording of a conversation (with the other person's permission) and listen to your own voice and word choices. Most people don't like listening to their own voice, but this practice will make you more aware of unprofessional vocabulary choices or unnecessary fillers you include without even noticing it. Do you begin every sentence with so or answer every question with absolutely? Stop it! One day I asked a friend who is excellent with vocabulary what words I used incorrectly, and she helped me improve my speaking. If you have the courage, do the same!

All-Star Space

Whether it's a corner office, cubical, or a tiny desk (is any desk ever big enough?), you have a space. A turf. Just like your apartment or house, just like your personal appearance, your office space should reflect pride in ownership. This is the place where you will log triumphs and grieve mistakes. It's where you will get news of your next promotion, and get cut down for your next mistake. Oh yes, that first day on the job can be fun when you set up your space and line up the rainbow of highlighters, straighten that pile of sticky notes, and arrange pictures of loved ones. But after a week or two, is your keyboard a little sticky and your plant a bit wilted? Thanks to researchers at the University of Arizona we know that your desk has fourteen times more germs than the office toilet seat. Ew.

Your desk is another opportunity to reflect your intelligence, detail orientation, and professional style. Every evening before you leave, take a good hard look at the disarray and dust surrounding your workspace. It's way too easy to become blind to our own messes and dirt! Make it a habit to at least stack papers in neat piles and corral stray pens before you leave. Then every Friday night without fail, clean off the desk completely, even if it means dumping papers into a drawer, and wipe things down. Refill your own printer paper and water your plants.

Here's why that is important. When someone comes to you with a task, they are sizing you up. They will notice if your wall calendar is two months behind and either think, "She must be really overworked. I better not ask her to participate," or "She sure doesn't pay attention to what's going on around her. I better not ask her to participate." Either way, it does not reflect well on you.

If your boss is approaching you with a problem, you have infinitely more credibility if your personal environment is clean and well-organized. If you are being accused of losing an important document and spill yesterday's Big Gulp as you spin around to rifle through the papers on the desk, you don't stand a chance. Even if the problem has nothing to do with missing papers, the person approaching with the complaint will find more justification to do so if your space appears in disarray.

It is also important for your own peace of mind. Have you ever prepped your house for sale? I'll never forget the first time I did and cleared off everything from the top of the counters. Each day I went into the kitchen, I felt a peace in how organized it looked. The same thing happens when you make your bed and the same thing happens when you come in on Monday to a cleared space.

Not everyone has the same standards for cleanliness—I get that. There is an important balance here, even in our frenzy to avoid germs. If you spend a half hour of company time wiping down your workstation every evening, you boss might have a reason to be unhappy. However, if you look around your immediate area right now and see more than one piece of junk mail or any dust (look hard), you need step up your game.

Any time you can steer an important conversation from a common area to the vicinity of your office space, you will have the upper hand. It's like a home game. It's your turf. It reminds coworkers and bosses alike that you already have important tasks and their request for help with the national meeting will have to be worked into your already busy schedule. It reminds the sales rep waiting to see your boss that you are the gatekeeper and not to be underestimated. It's a subtle psychological advantage, but subtlety is the name of the game for an all-star admin.

You may want to consider a gimmick for your space. Now I'm not suggesting wear a unicorn outfit on Halloween and sprinkle glitter around your nameplate—because I'm already doing that. But you need to find something. You want to create a favorable and memorable impression when someone spends time near your desk. A simple and useful idea is to have a silly-face stress ball handy and encourage people to give it a good squeeze (then disinfect it, of course).

Another possibility is to hand out de-motivational sayings. Sayings like: "Some people dream of success; other people live to crush those dreams," or "Procrastination: Hard work pays off after time, but laziness pays off today." They are a funny way to break the ice and build rapport with new people you encounter. You may want to keep some chocolate hidden in your desk to use at the right time. It does become expensive to be the office supplier of chocolate, but you might find that person who will need to get past the 3 p.m. slump (and that person might even be you). See how it works? You can also use inspirational quotes as long as you change them out. Otherwise, they just become part of the scenery that no one, including yourself, notices.

There are a thousand more ways to use your turf as a source of positivity, encouragement, or humor so I thought I'd name some for you:

- Put a selection of pens in a cup with fun toppers
- Display a dinosaur pen holder
- Use funny (but not potentially offensive) notepads
- Use a creative mouse pad
- Make a sign that reads, "Smile, you are on camera."

You will have to pick and choose what might work in your environment and make sure you don't overdo it. You could always have a drawer of fun things to display and rotate them out.

Hot Tip: More than one boss? Display a white board or sticky note calendar with all your current assignments. Your bosses may look at the lists and think twice before giving you something they can do themselves.

All-Star Conflict Management

It is only natural to disagree with others—conflict management is just a part of communication. The problem is most of us consider ourselves pretty good at communication. We talk and write emails all day, right? The truth is, most of us need to hone those basic communication skills at least a bit. There are times when you need to get your point across and must be heard, and there are times to let it go. How do you know which is which?

Bible students and fans of ancient proverbs recognize the phrase "don't cast your pearls before swine." I like that word picture when considering how and when to expend energy on conflict. How do you know whether or not it will be a waste of time to push back? Some people think they just can't be wrong. They thrive on arguments and are truthfully too insecure to ever consider their opinion might not be the best.

The biggest secret a deft arguer has is to get the other person off track as soon as possible. You will be in an argument or discussion and then before you know it, you are talking about something different than the original subject. It is a great technique that is very annoying. If you are paying attention, you will hear right when it happens. As soon as you recognize the subject has changed, get back on track. Whatever he says that is not part of the original point, say something like, "We can talk about that next, but first let's discuss (subject)." You may have to use this technique several times and possibly always with this person. However, you will be heard and will not be lured away into another discussion before you are ready.

How do you know if you are argumentative? Wait, what? You thought this section would be all about how you could live with those people who create drama at the office. If you haven't figured it out yet, this book has a lot about self-awareness. Are you an arguer? Do you listen to what the other person has to say and actually consider her opinion? Can you accept it when you are proven wrong, or do you just get annoyed? If you can't remember the last time you made a mistake you might be one of those who just knows you are always right. Not good.

How about trying to understand someone else's position so well that you could argue for it. Here's an exercise you can do. Take any big opinion you have on any topic. It can even be a hot-button issue like immigration or socialized medicine. Can you argue for the other side? Can you say why you'd be for or against something and defend it so well that I couldn't tell what you believed? If so, you have really considered the issues. If not, you haven't. It's pretty simple.

Here's an example: Let's say my coworker wants to schedule an event at XYZ Hotel. My experience with the customer service at that venue has been terrible, and I let her know I think it is a poor choice. But she presses the point, and I continue to listen. Turns out, the hotel had dropped prices, was under new management, and had glowing recent reviews. If I let my feelings get hurt when she doesn't take my opinion as gospel, things could go south. But if I ask myself, "What if she's right?" we can move forward with good results. Before starting a conflict, always consider what it would look like if the other person were, in fact, right.

Let's touch on listening a bit more. You have to listen. Not only that, but you have to listen to understand rather than just to hear. Make every conversation, no matter how you feel, a discussion. Try to wrap your mind around what the conflict is really about, and stay on track. Project's late? Then why are you talking about last week when she forgot to save that important document? What good is that doing to help get the project done?

THE ALL-STAR ADMINISTRATIVE PROFESSIONAL

Finally, you don't have to say something about everything. Why not just let some things go? I remember speaking for a group and a woman said she gets so frustrated because there is a coworker who will not close cabinet doors. Sure, I can see how that might be frustrating, but it doesn't have to be. Is it that big of a deal that an occasional cabinet is left open? Ask yourself why it bothers you. And when you say something, it doesn't have to be a big deal. "Hey Martha, could you close that cabinet?" Rinse and repeat as necessary. Not only will life get easier around the office, but your stress level will go down.

Hot tip: Keep track for a day or two of how many times you argue. Just make a hashmark on a notepad or on your phone. At the end of the day ask yourself if it was worth risking your health and possibly your job to get your point across. Then do this exercise for a week and see if you can bring your average down. It's all about self-awareness.

All-Star Confidence

Do you have all-star confidence? Most of us don't. We have those little voices who say we aren't good enough and can't achieve what we want. And we spend too much time wondering what people think of us. The thoughts and behaviors from a lack of confidence keep us from living the life we want.

That's why I developed an online coaching program called "In Confidence", which has been a huge difference maker in the lives of women. Confidence is foundational to success in any industry, at any level, for any gender. If you are not confident, you will not succeed. Sounds like a downer, but the good news is that if you exercise confidence, success will come more easily! So what does that look like in the life of an administrative professional?

It means sharing some of your great ideas for organizing the office or the systems that are used. And when or if your ideas are not used, it means not falling apart, but continuing to push forward for change. More confidence means you have better work relationships because you are not afraid to have conversations with coworkers and vendors. Your greater confidence means you are able to set boundaries with your boss and others to get the respect you deserve. Strong boundaries mean others can count on you, but not take advantage of you.

Confidence is not arrogance, so you are a helper, not a hinderer to others' success. The ability to admit mistakes and press forward, capitalize on your strengths, continue to learn and grow and have a good time while doing it, is all about confidence. Overall, a confident admin has a better job and life.

Confidence coaching is not a temporary fix. When you change your view of yourself it sets you on a completely new path. Let me give you three different real-life examples of women whose boost in confidence changed their lives:

- Stephanie was so timid when she came to see me that she couldn't even voice her opinion about what to have for dinner. She simply didn't think she was good enough to make good choices. She second-guessed every word and move she made to the point she was afraid at the thought of saying "hi" to a stranger in the grocery store. So what did I ask her to do? Say "hi" to five strangers! And, guess what, she did it! Stephanie walked right out of her comfort zone during many other exercises and learned to assert herself (including saying "no" when appropriate). The more choices she made, the stronger she got. She began to realize she was good enough. In the end, her husband even thanked me for giving him back his wife—although he adored her no matter what, he regained a healthy life partner when she made the decision to attack her lack of confidence head-on.
- Kathy wanted to run a marathon, but managed to sabotage herself at every turn. That's where I came in. I not only held her accountable to her rigorous physical training routine, I taught her to train her mind to think healthy thoughts. She was enough! She just needed to teach herself to believe it. Guess what—Kathy rocked that marathon. And she didn't stop there. Today she has a lively social media presence encouraging others to set and attain their own goals.
- One of my favorite success stories is Judith. To the outside observer, she had it all—money, looks, family, smarts. But Judith did not like herself. She was constantly using negative self-talk like "You're stupid," or "You're clumsy." Although she

was highly educated and successful in her career, she was too focused on her faults to create the life she truly wanted. Confidence coaching helped her to shine a light on the truth that she was not stupid, or clumsy, but was in fact poised, intelligent, and a true gift to the world. That set her on a path to start her own business. She credits confidence coaching for improving her life.

If you feel lacking in confidence in any way, join the club. While speaking to groups around the country I have heard the stories of women just like you and me. Women who have good lives, but still lack confidence in areas where they need it. Most of your friends, if not all, have a sense they are not good enough and may even have imposter syndrome. This is the feeling that you have gotten to where you are in life because of dumb luck and not because of your talent, skills, and perseverance. One recent study showed that 70 percent of people experience imposter syndrome at some point. I've been there and that's why I'm dedicated to helping women have more confidence and more of what they want in life. You can be a success story yourself—and luck has very little to do with it!

Hot Tip: If you want to be more confident, hang out with confident people. Watch how they speak, how they spend their time—really try to figure out what makes them tick. Then apply it to your own life. Maybe even ask them to help you identify some practical goals and to encourage you to meet them. If you are confident by nature, find someone to mentor. Be the change!

A Note About the Difficult Boss

It's hard to be an all-star with a difficult boss, but you can do it! The biggest key is to get to know his or her preferences. One admin I know with a difficult boss said she would send him an email and he would send it back telling her that the subject line was not capitalized the way he wanted. Oh my gosh! Seriously. That's difficult. She said this was just one of many examples. So, you may ask, how did she handle working for him? She did things exactly as he required as soon as she found out what he wanted. After just a short time, he commented that she was the best assistant he ever had. She didn't resist just because what he wanted was, honestly, a bit silly.

Another key is to watch for particular times of the day when your boss is in a certain mood. Think of when you were a teenager and you timed exactly when to ask your parents for money. You didn't just ask any time you felt like it; you watched their moods and what they were doing. It's the same with the difficult boss. Perhaps she isn't the nicest before her coffee or perhaps right after lunch she's too busy to be bothered. Pay attention and you will have the timing down before long.

Recently, I spoke for a company that had an extremely toxic boss. Thankfully, each time I spoke there I had a small group, so they felt comfortable sharing specifics with me and getting advice. Oh, my goodness, I am not sure I could have stayed under the circumstances, but they felt they had no choice. This boss was not only a yeller, which is bad enough, but a screamer, and a forgetter.

She would tell them to do something and then forget she told them to do it and later have them do the opposite. Then when they didn't do the first thing, she got very mad. Wow, that's tough. One coworker shared what she did was make sure she got everything possible in email to keep a record. Then she communicated with her boss as much as she could in writing. And if that isn't a possibility with you, keep a notebook with dates and carry it around. It seems like a big pain, but it might save you from the forgetting type of boss. Each time you are given a project, write down the specifics and the date and time you were given the instructions. And when I say time, I mean exact time, as in 2:54. This is a strategy I learned from a professional who might need to show his notes in court. Using 2:54 sounds more truthful than 3:00 and we don't want it to just sound more truthful, but to be completely truthful. When you read to your boss from your notebook, "Last Tuesday, at 2:54, you told me to prioritize the Wilson campaign," she is more likely to understand you are telling the truth.

If you have a difficult boss, chances are good that she is a yeller. It is the most common complaint I have heard of when speaking to administrative professionals. My advice is to not yell back or be confrontational in that moment in any way. This even means your facial expressions need to be in check. Right now you have to make a decision. Can you muster up the confidence it will take to talk to her about it? If you absolutely refuse to handle this situation are you okay to let it continue? You have to decide—I cannot do it for you. Most people choose to ignore their issues and hope they will go away, or decide to be passive-aggressive. From experience I know that these techniques do not work. People do not get hints and problems don't disappear when we are dealing with challenging people. You have to stand up for yourself if anything is to change. I want to encourage you to do just that.

If you choose to have that tough conversation, wait about 10 minutes after the confrontation to allow yourself time to cool off. Then make a plan of what to say and go into her office and close the door. These conversations work best if not done by appointment but handled as quickly as possible once tempers have calmed. It should be eye to eye so make sure you are sitting if she is. Feel free to use your notes. Lean in just a bit and use steady eye contact. Speak in an even tone and tell her you need to talk to her for two minutes and need her full attention. And this should only take two minutes or under. You need to be very succinct, and that is why notes are useful. There is nothing wrong with referring to them, as needed. Use "I" language and tell her how you feel and that you need her to communicate in a different way.

Do not use the words "yell" or "yelling" or "screaming" which might increase her defensive posture. Be strong and act like this does not intimidate you or make you nervous.

Here is a sample conversation:

"Hello Sarah. I need to speak to you for just two minutes. I feel like I'm not respected when you raise your voice to me. In the future I need you to tell me what I've done wrong in a different way, and I'm going to do everything I can to make your job easier."

Pause. At this point, look at her demeanor. Does she seem like she is apologetic, or does she seem to be getting angry? If she seems apologetic, give her time to speak. If she seems to be getting angry, just thank her for her time and leave.

This may need to be repeated and if so, use the same language and technique the next time. You decide how many times is acceptable before you go above her head. If you ever have to go above her head, discuss this with HR first.

Here is how that could go:

"Sarah, we have had three conversations about the way you speak to me. (Refer to your notes and read this next part.) One was the 5th at 1:36 p.m., the second on the 8th at 2:32 p.m., and the third was this morning at 9:02

a.m. I spoke to Jennifer in HR a few minutes ago because I am not sure how to handle this anymore. Out of respect for you, I wanted to let you know."

These types of conversations are not easy, but are necessary. Doesn't just reading this make you want to cringe a bit? The good news is that you get to decide your own boundaries and what you will tolerate. The really good news is your courage may eventually make things better for everyone at your company.

If there is no HR or if she is the boss, you have a problem. (Like I have to tell you?) Stay firm and set your boundaries. One woman I met while speaking said her boss was the top boss and screamed and cursed at her often. She also shared she lived in a small town and she hadn't found any other work options. I gave her tools for setting boundaries, but there are truly times you feel there are no choices and I get that. However, thinking about what he did to her psyche has me boiling and the stress of it all may actually shorten her life. If this describes your situation, do everything you can to find another way to make a living. Life is too short to allow workplace stress to negatively affect your health.

Hot Tip: If your boss gives you one more thing to do at the end of the day, state firmly and respectfully: "This will take me 30 minutes to complete. Would you like me to stay and get overtime or do it in the morning?" Another strategy to follow when your boss gives you a task you really don't have time for is to confidently show him your priority list. This helps him see how busy you are and oftentimes, he will take something off your plate.

Conclusion

Do you want to be an all-star in your profession? Who doesn't! I say, start preparing your acceptance speech for the Administrative Assistant Hall of Fame right now. You can see how doable each step in the process is and I know you can take those steps, starting today.

Many of the admins I have met over the years tell me sometimes they get tired of not being in charge. Sometimes they want to make the big decisions and have all the control. I'll let you in on a little secret—you have all the control. You control your attitude, appearance, brand, projects, relationships, space, and confidence. You may not control your boss or that circle talker across the hall, but you have all the power to create good boundaries.

Take a brutally honest look at your goals, needs, lifestyle, habits, and thoughts. Surround yourself with people who bring out the best in you. Focus on physical, mental, spiritual, and emotional health. Give. Love. Serve. And work hard.

It takes planning, long days, sacrifice, and maybe even a few uncomfortable chats with coworkers or bosses, but there is nothing more satisfying than being at the top of your game. Being in control. Being an all-star. I know you can do it.

About the Author

A gifted keynote speaker, award-winning author, corporate trainer and personal coach, Dr. Susan Harrison has helped thousands of people all over the world develop effective business and life skills. Her areas of expertise include confidence building and de-stressing, along with various facets of personal and professional development. With disarming transparency, Susan shares her struggles and successes in work and personal communications. Susan is a 2018-2019 inductee into the International Association of Women Influencer of the Year Circle. In 2017, she earned Maverick of the Year (Bronze) Stevie Award for Women in Business. She is the 2016 Award Winner of the Readers' Favorite Excellence in Writing International Contest, and also a seasoned media professional after appearing on numerous local and national broadcasts.

To book Dr. Harrison for your next event, contact her at susan@drsusanharrison.com. Her fun, energetic delivery and fast-paced, interactive sessions will leave you wanting more.

For more information, visit drsusanharrison.com.